London Transport 1970–84

Bus Operations

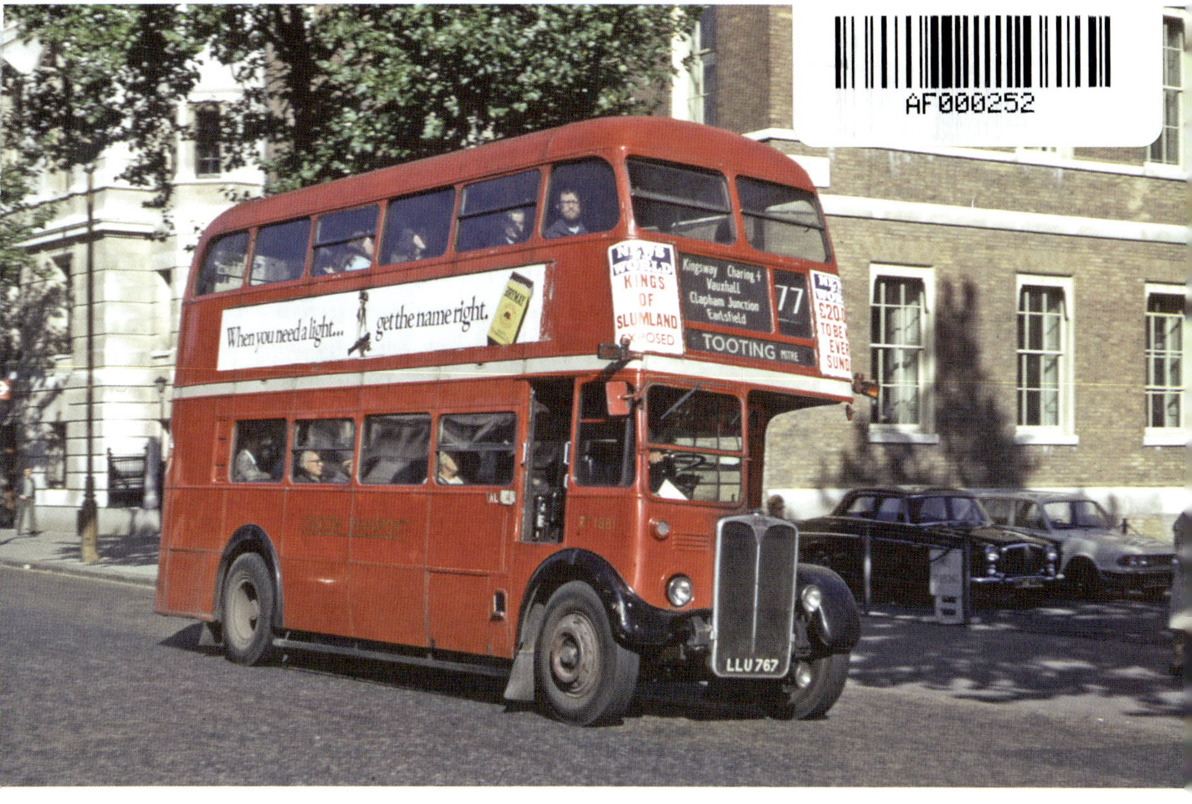

MATTHEW WHARMBY AND R. C. RILEY

KEY Books

BRITAIN'S BUSES SERIES, VOLUME 7

Front cover image: Throughout the period covered by this book, the venerable Routemaster continued to exemplify London's bus network; maybe not at its best, but nowhere near its worst. On 28 October 1983 Wandsworth's RM 639 (WLT 639) lays over opposite its home garage.

Back cover image: For a variety of reasons, the DMS family of Daimler Fleetline had far less success in the capital despite their custom specification. Examples like DMS 174 (JGF 174K), seen at Blackfriars on 13 June 1974, lasted barely a decade in service.

Title page image: RT 1881 (LLU 767) lent its fleetnumber to the star of Summer Holiday, but on 2 October 1973 the real one was still going, allocated to Merton and operating the 77 route down Whitehall.

Contents page image: Coming into its own after trolleybus routes 654 and 657 finished, the 157 could never seem to settle after the closure of Carshalton garage, wandering around between any combination of Sutton, Merton, Thornton Heath and Croydon. RT 2199 (KGU 128) was a Sutton bus when photographed in October 1972 at Crystal Palace, seeing out the last few months of crew operation. After the inevitable arrival of DMSs, this bus moved on by year's end to Plumstead, from where it was withdrawn in October 1975 and sold to Wombwell Diesels the following February.

First published in 2013 as *London Transport 1970-1984* by Ian Allan.

This edition published in 2021 by Key Books.

Key Books
An imprint of Key Publishing Ltd
PO Box 100
Stamford
Lincs PE19 1XQ

www.keypublishing.com

Copyright © Matt Wharmby, 2013

ISBN 978 1 913870 34 8

Unless otherwise stated, all photographs are the copyright of R. C. Riley.

All rights reserved. Reproduction in whole or in part in any form whatsoever or by any means is strictly prohibited without the prior permission of the Publisher.

Typeset by SJmagic DESIGN SERVICES, India.

Contents

Introduction		4
Chapter 1	RTs	5
Chapter 2	Routemasters	22
Chapter 3	XAs and FRM 1	40
Chapter 4	DMSs and MDs	42
Chapter 5	Metrobuses and Titans	62
Chapter 6	RFs	74
Chapter 7	Merlins and Swifts	78
Chapter 8	MSs and LSs	88
Chapter 9	BSs and BLs	94
Chapter 10	FSs	95
Chapter 11	Beyond	96

Introduction

R. C. (Dick) Riley (1921-2006) was one of the country's foremost railway photographers, whose vast and carefully composed output over several decades has graced a score of books and magazines.

As well as cataloguing Britain's vanishing steam operations and their replacement by diesel and electric locomotives, Dick also turned his camera on his local buses. Living for many years in Beckenham, which is shared between Greater London and west Kent, he recorded meticulously the passage of time that saw the time-honoured London Transport red buses give way to those of independent companies.

In other books, it's the 'specials' – advertising liveries, strange workings, vanity routes – that have tended to hog the limelight, leaving no room for the common-or-garden vehicles, the unsung heroes that demand no glamour or special recognition. This small selection captures those everyday buses of London Transport at the close of its glory days, spanning roughly the years 1970, when three thousand RTs were still in service and one-man-operation was only just beginning, to 1984, right before the capital was changed forever by tendering and devolution.

Matthew Wharmby
July, 2012

Since one-man-operation, and its purpose-built vehicles, were failing so dramatically during the 1970s, a quarter of the DMS intake was revised to enter service as crew-operated buses. MCW-bodied DM 1746 (GHM 746N) was one of a large number of DMs to replace RTs at Holloway in 1975, but would barely make it into the 1980s. It is seen from atop Holborn Viaduct in August 1977; the MD-class Metropolitan behind is also a crew bus.

Chapter 1

RTs

Simple, tough, reliable and supremely versatile, the RT family lasted for forty years as the shining example of standardisation at its best. No other single authority has come even close to fielding anywhere like seven thousand essentially identical vehicles or enjoyed the image of quality and reliability that that ideal bestowed.

By 1970, even after the withdrawal of the RTW and RTL classes and the hiving off of the Country Area's green buses to the NBC as London Country, London Transport could still field nearly three thousand RTs, which could be found scattered round the system anywhere the observer chose to look. Routemasters had thinned their numbers but failed to take them out of the game entirely, and nor would the subsequent intake of Merlins, Swifts and DMSs. Still, withdrawals were steady, and even though a late revival forced many RTs to be recertified to cover for failing examples of younger generations of buses, by 1978 the writing was on the wall. To a crowd of thousands, RT 624 made its final approach to Barking garage on route 62 at 1.45 pm on the afternoon of Saturday 7 April 1979.

Sutton's RT 358 (HLX 175) reposes outside its home garage after a rounder on the 213A on 30 August 1971. This bus had only been based here a month and would not linger, passing to Walworth after the pair of routes 213 and 213A were converted to DMS OMO on 5 August 1972. Subsequent transfers would take it to Brixton, Streatham, Catford and Southall, from where it was withdrawn in May 1977 and sold immediately for scrap.

ABOVE: The classic stand at Chislehurst War Memorial has been the terminal for the 161 family for many generations, the route(s) probing out in all three possible directions over the years but always falling back to rest here. One day in March 1972 we see both 161 and 161A immortalised, in the persona of RT 1938 (LUC 18) and RT 627 (JXC 435). The former RT is an Abbey Wood motor, allocated there since May 1971 but to end its life at Plumstead in November 1977, while the latter, a Sidcup bus, was days from withdrawal and did not survive the crusher.

OPPOSITE: Sutton's modernisation had taken place in two stages during 1953 – first with the replacement of its Ds by RTLs, and straight after that came RTs to take over the garage's entire double-deck roster. Stability ensued, and by 17 July 1972, when RT 2669 (LYR 653) was captured at Wimbledon, the 93 had been RT-operated for 19 years, the route changing not at all other than for the removal of its North Cheam-Epsom section in favour of curtailment behind the GLC border, and thus does it remain today. The bus was withdrawn in January 1975, while the 93 was converted to RM on 25 March 1976. Six generations of buses have followed – RMs, DMs/DMSs, Ms, NVs, EVLs and now DOEs.

ABOVE: Tram routes 26 and 31 begat bus routes 168 and 170, and neither was exempt from dwindling fortunes as passengers generally deserted buses for cars. By 17 July 1972, when Stockwell's RT 2306 (KGU 335) was pictured making its way down Whitehall, the 168 reached its Farringdon Street terminus only during peak hours and didn't operate at all on Sundays. The bus transferred away even before Routemasters reached the route, spending most of the years 1973 and 1974 at Barking before withdrawal in November. The 168 lasted not that much longer itself, being taken off in 1981.

OPPOSITE: Historically a Sidcup-operated route, the 229 nonetheless had support from Bexleyheath between 1964 and 1977, and it is this garage's RT 2921 (MLL 668) that is seen in its home region on 7 April 1973. It had come from Leyton on transfer the previous October and would remain at Bexleyheath for the rest of its London career, withdrawal coming in December 1975. It was not until 21 May 1977 that the 229 received Routemasters.

London Transport 1970–84

ABOVE: For such a prestige number, the 1 has consistently failed to live up to expectations, tending to skirt the more obvious centres of population rather than probing directly into them, though for a time it did provide useful links from north-west to south-east London. Perhaps accordingly, it was to take until 1975 before the route was converted from RT to RM, and for posterity, in anticipation of that change, Dick Riley recorded the passage through Baker Street of New Cross's RT 3407 (LYR 626) on 21 February 1974. This bus moved on to Barking in September 1974 and managed to stay there until April 1978, making it to within a year of the end of the RT class.

OPPOSITE: On 27 September 1973 heavy construction work is taking place on the northernmost end of London Bridge, forcing routes like the 21 to mount a ramp. Sidcup's RT 939 (JXN 329) has just done so and can now resume its long trek southeastwards with, hopefully, no more drama. Unusually for such a long trunk route, the 21 was RT-operated until March 1975; RT 939 departed Sidcup nine months before that date and saw further service at Bromley, Norbiton and Barking. The conversion of the penultimate RT route, the 87, to Routemaster on 28 October 1978 at last occasioned its withdrawal.

London Transport 1970–84

ABOVE: Although done with the kindest of intentions, putting a roof over wide open bus stations merely channels the airstream into howling gales that batter the bodies stood miserably therein, and thus did passengers waiting for buses suffer at London Bridge for nearly forty years. On 4 June 1974 Brixton's RT 489 (HLX 306) is passing through on the 133; unusually, this bus's intermediate blind box has been masked to take a 'KK' panel from a Routemaster. It had been transferred to Brixton the previous month but would leave in May 1975 following the conversion of the 133 to DM operation; it lasted until August 1978, seemingly escaping route after route as they lost their RTs for RMs.

OPPOSITE: The 86's long slog up and down the Romford Road between Limehouse and Romford was by 1974 the province of twenty RTs from Seven Kings. On 7 May that year RT 2851 (LYF 498) ambles through Bromley-by-Bow. Seven Kings was its final garage, the bus serving there from March 1973 to April 1976, in which month the 86 completed its conversion to RM.

ABOVE: It was seen as either reassuring or alarming that by 1975 the first thing travellers into Heathrow were likely to see as they stepped out of the airport was an RT, still working on routes 105 and 140. Harrow Weald had been scheduled to receive RMs very early on in the process of RT-to-RM conversions, but it was not until 15 July 1978 that this finally happened, making the 140 London Transport's fourth-last RT-operated service. On 22 July 1974 RT 4800 (NXP 942) is negotiating its way past comprehensive rebuilding of the airport periphery.

OPPOSITE: The grand tour of the USA and Canada accomplished by three RTs in 1952 was by 1974 a distant memory, but one bus of the trio remained in service – albeit under a different identity thanks to the vagaries of the overhauling system. Poplar's RT 1708 (KYY 535), seen at Aldgate straying from its normal route 277A duty to RM-operated 40A on 22 May 1974, was now host to the Park Royal body (6350) with the unique semi-circular roof dome vents, having been outshopped with it after overhaul in January 1969; until then RT 2776 had always managed to hold on to its identity. RT 1708 was withdrawn in December 1974 and scrapped the following March.

ABOVE: One would think that the comparatively untroubled 118 route, ambling through various unexciting parts of south London on its way between Morden and Clapham Common, would have been an early candidate for OMO, but it wasn't one-manned until 1985. It wasn't until 14 December 1975 that its RTs were replaced by RMs, and on 23 August of that year, Brixton's RT 528 (HLX 345) is caught heading south along Streatham High Road. This bus lingered at Brixton a little beyond the 118's conversion to RM, but left when the much more ambitious 109 route commenced its own conversion and hopped from garage to garage during the next two years, finally coming out of service at Catford in March 1978.

OPPOSITE: After a quarter of a century of unbroken RT operation (with interludes where fit by RTWs and RTLs), the long and sinuous 109 route snaking down the Brighton Road finally fell due for conversion to RM operation. The Brixton allocation went over first, from 23 May 1976, the Thornton Heath allocation of nearly equal size succumbing on 3 October. RT 394 (HLX 211) was one of the former's buses, and had gained fame by being the last RT to be outshopped from Aldenham overhaul in February 1970. Allocated to Brixton since November 1971, this shot sees it in the South Croydon area on 6 October 1975; its subsequent transfer to Walthamstow in August 1976 was to be its last, and it would be withdrawn the following January.

ABOVE: On 23 July 1977 both 139 and 148 succumbed to DMS OMO; perhaps a little later than may have been the case, had Seven Kings garage not needed to undergo comprehensive rebuilding so that it could accommodate vehicles of larger dimensions than RTs. On 13 March 1976, at the Dagenham terminus shared by both routes, are Seven Kings's RT 4215 (LYF 274) and RT 4126 (LUC 475).

OPPOSITE: Introduced in 1956 to link the residents of the Woodlands Estate on Plumstead Common with shops and jobs in Woolwich, the 192 expanded quickly with an extension to Lewisham. Neither Catford nor New Cross garages, which inherited responsibility for the service and shared it between themselves, were particularly close to the roads served, thus RT 1060 (JXN 88) would have had to work up to Lewisham from its home (Catford) out of service. Catford was this bus's last posting, withdrawal coming in August 1977.

London Transport 1970–84

ABOVE: Probably the most attractive terminus on the entire London Transport red-bus network, Downe was where the 146 turned around. Despite fielding just two buses, they had to remain RTs all the way to 22 April 1978 as nothing since built would fit down the narrow country lanes to the south of Bromley and Keston. Eventually Bristol LHs of BL class were purchased for just this reason, and a host of routes with width restrictions succumbed similarly. On 28 February 1977 Bromley's RT 3490 (LYR 909) reposes in winter sunshine; it would be withdrawn in August and sold to Wombwell Diesels in September.

OPPOSITE: The 176, already famous for being the host of the last RTL in 1968, became the last route to operate the RT class through the heart of central London. Still shared between Willesden and Walworth at either end, it would be converted to RM on 11 March 1976; on 25 February RT 4638 (NXP 891) is sighted at Charing Cross with a side blind all it is able to muster for information, together with a chalked number.

Chapter 2
Routemasters

Little more needs said about what came to be known as London's quintessential bus, so why not let the pictures do the talking. Even the cession of 209 green examples to London Country as the period covered by this book opens does not exempt them from coverage, as very nearly all of them would come straight back by the end of the decade, urgently needed to repair services from the failings of DMs. Thus the fleet remained broadly intact until the aftermath of the Fares Fair debacle; September 1982 saw 200 RMs taken out of service, and withdrawals would accelerate as mass one-manning resumed. The book leaves off with the type seemingly doomed, but we all know by now that in 1984 the Routemaster was by no means out for the count.

ABOVE: Cricklewood's RM 1725 (725 DYE) seems to have Victoria Bus Station to itself as it sets off for Neasden on 26 November 1973. Conversion to crew-DMS was imminent, but Routemasters would be back seven years later. The 16's arrow-straight path up the Edgware Road has been chopped back successively over the years, getting no further north now than Cricklewood Garage, but RM 1725 managed to sidestep all those alterations and lasted all the way till June 2004, only succumbing when its last route, Brixton's 137, was converted to OPO.

OPPOSITE: Perhaps London's quintessential bus route, the 11 is proof that the tourist of the 1970s didn't need to spend huge quantities of coin on dedicated services when all the attractions he could wish to see could be enjoyed from atop a route 11 RM. Conversion from RTW had been accomplished in February 1966, and on 7 June 1973 Dalston's RM 971 (WLT 971) is seen at St Paul's, opposite RM 2021 on the 9. RM 971 didn't make it past the first swathe of Routemaster withdrawals in September 1982 and was broken up at Aldenham by Vic Berry.

London Transport 1970–84

ABOVE: On a rainy 12 February 1976 RM 1665 (665 DYE) is seen working through New Cross. Peckham's 36 group branched off at this point to three separate destinations: the majority 36B to Grove Park via Lewisham and Catford, while the main 36 went to Hither Green and the 36A probed south to Brockley Rise, but only in the peak hours. The routes were rationalised in the early 1990s and the 36A came off without replacement, while RM 1665 was one of the unfortunate first two hundred to be withdrawn when the post-Fares Fair cuts bit on 4 September 1982; it did not last the year out.

OPPOSITE: Spring is in the air as Peckham's RM 1622 (622 DYE) works through Blackfriars on 4 April 1974, albeit only as far as Honor Oak, a little to the north of the 63's historic Crystal Palace terminus, and indeed pulled back to that point permanently in 2003. The 63's next few years comprised six years of crew-operated Metropolitans, RMs back for three years and then a straight conversion to OPO with Titans, which operated until 2000 with stragglers able to be sighted until 2003. RM 1622 was withdrawn from Catford in September 1982, as one of the first to go, and was broken up by Vic Berry on site at Aldenham.

The operation of RMAs on stage service was a curious interlude that underscored the sheer desperation of the spares shortage of the mid-1970s. The first thirteen such Routemasters were bought back from BEA and pressed into service very much 'as is', with just a slipboard alerting route 175's passengers to the fact. On 13 March 1976 North Street's RMA 9 (NMY 646E) is captured at a very bleak-looking Dagenham stand. After the emergency had passed, RTs would return to the 175 and be replaced by RMs in due course. RMA 9 became Catford's staff bus and spent a decade taking its personnel to and from Aldenham; it survives today with Timebus.

On 14 May 1976 Camberwell's RM 2026 (ALM 26B) is chased round Parliament Square by DM 1147 (KUC 147P), just put into service at Chalk Farm on the 24. DM operation wouldn't last on the 24, but Routemasters would remain on the 3 all the way through the 1980s and into the first three days of 1993. RM 2026 was withdrawn from Merton in February 1987 and exported to Japan.

ABOVE: It took perhaps longer than might have been expected for the entire RML class to be put to their best intended use by being concentrated on central London routes, but the 6 was one such route that had RMLs from new. Nearly eleven years on from that conversion from RM is Hackney's RML 2487 (JJD 487D) at Mansion House during July 1976. Both bus and route would expire in the same year, RML 2487 being withdrawn from Shepherd's Bush (by that time of London United) in January 2004 and the 6 going OPO that 27 March.

OPPOSITE: Going only as far west as Kensington when espied at Mansion House one August 1977 lunchtime, Dalston's RM 2001 (ALM 1B) exists today only in numberplate form. Not particularly valuable as what later came to be known as a 'cherished' registration other than from its low number, this mark spent fifteen years on Titan T 1000 and now adorns an Audi A4. RM 2001 itself ended up as a BUSCO-equipped Routemaster for the 36 group and was withdrawn from Peckham in April 1987, at which point it gave up its registration and departed for scrapping.

London Transport 1970–84

Routemasters

ABOVE: Allocated new to Norwood in November 1964, by 9 March 1978 RM 2057 (ALM 57B) was still there, although of course by now a different combination of body and chassis just wearing the RM 2057 identity and tax disc. It is setting off from Crystal Palace on the 2B, but not all the way to Golders Green as the route otherwise did.

OPPOSITE: The visitor to London with bus photography on his mind can make no better start than simply coming out of the side entrance to Waterloo station and turning his camera upon the healthy number of buses to be found heading south. Dick Riley was there on 11 August 1977 and captured, amongst other vehicles, Croydon's RM 634 (WLT 634) on the 68, a quarter of the way through its long slog to its home base. This Routemaster lasted in service until 1985, by which time it was working from Finchley, and was scrapped shortly after.

Catford's RM 915 (WLT 915) passes through its home region on a sunny spring day, 23 April 1978. Historically operated by Catford, the 180 had from 1963 been joined by Abbey Wood, and from then until the opening of the new Plumstead garage they shared the route. RM 915 last operated out of Victoria, leaving service in February 1986.

The terminus of the once-mighty 2 route at West Norwood, Rosendale, was hardly a major passenger objective, but since 1970 the 2B had taken over the impetus southward to Crystal Palace. Eventually the 2 withered away to little more than a local shuttle and was taken off in 1992, but by then the likes of RM 1728 (728 DYE) and RM 1340 (340 CLT) had long gone. The former was withdrawn from Tottenham in October 1984 and scrapped in 1986, while the latter didn't make it past the first tranche of withdrawals in September 1982 and was also broken up.

One of the less welcome changes of the 1970s, amongst other things, was the quite unnecessary replacement of classic gold-leaf fleetnumbers and fleetnames with stark white versions. Application was fairly quick, it taking only seven years to treat the whole fleet (RTs exempted, while they were still in service). RM 1128 (128 CLT), allocated to Peckham by 1981, was the last, and in this 17 August 1981 shot at Victoria it looks dusty but not dirty. This bus would be withdrawn from Victoria in March 1990 and scrapped in June.

The time-honoured Oxford Circus stand of the 113 has only just been retired, but by the time Routemasters were operating on this trunk service it was the northern end to Edgware that was starting to come under threat. In any case, RML 2605 (NML 605E) is occupying the other side of John Prince's Street when captured on 17 August 1981; perhaps the stand was already taken. Looking very smart, this bus would survive until four months from the end, when it was withdrawn from Putney on 22 July 2005. That makes it, despite its vintage, the most recently-experienced bus in these pages!

London Transport 1970–84

ABOVE: First off the production lines after the small batch of 24 thirty-footers, RM 904 (WLT 904) entered service from Finchley in January 1962. By 31 March 1982 it was a Bromley bus allocated to the 94, which had been Routemaster-operated for just over three years but which was set to disappear with the 4 September changes, split into two services. It is caught at traffic lights by Grove Park station; withdrawal was from Stamford Hill in August 1986.

OPPOSITE: On 31 March 1982 Upton Park's RML 2544 (JJD 544D) operates through Tower Hill on the 23. The classic red buses of London Transport have never needed to draw attention to themselves, but towards the end of 1983 route 23's buses and roadside infrastructure were selected for dedicated advertising that would draw the punters to the Tower, the most important tourist attraction served by this Upton Park-operated RML route. In a controversial change of plans in 1985 the 23 was withdrawn and reconfigured into an expanded 15, with similar branding, while RML 2544 survived to form part of the 73's final Routemaster complement, passing thence to Clapton (also Arriva London North by then) where it saw out its days on the 38 on 28 October 2005.

London Transport 1970–84

At the time of this March 1983 shot the 12 was still the longest route in London, four garages operating it with RMs. For Elmers End, the 12 was its bread and butter, RM 1228 (228 CLT) being just one of a sizeable number allocated. The garage closed on 25 October 1986 and RM 1228 was transferred to Camberwell, from where it was withdrawn in September 1988 and scrapped more or less immediately.

Streatham's RM 1063 (63 CLT) looks pristine as it rests in its home garage on 13 February 1984. The garage would be closed for refurbishment that October, to be reopened on 7 February 1987 but falling victim to the recession of the early 1990s and closing permanently on 14 March 1992. The Routemaster was withdrawn from Norwood in March 1987 but survives in preservation today.

Chapter 3
XAs and FRM 1

One class an experimental series purchased to determine the suitability of rear-engined buses for London's exacting conditions, the other a cherished one-off that should have gone into production, but was squashed by Leyland. Very much products of their time, the Atlanteans attempted to convince London that rear-engined buses were the way forward; LT was far from convinced despite the ongoing staff shortage making it impossible to fulfil existing schedules with universal two-man operation. While evaluating the XAs (and accompanying XF class of Daimler Fleetlines) on a mix of central, suburban and Country Area routes, LT was working on its own advanced design based on the Routemaster but sending its engine to the back. Neither XA nor FRM class could be said to have fulfilled the best intentions of their operator; the former were taken out of service en masse in 1973 and sold to Hong Kong, while the FRM bumbled round Potters Bar on its own one-bus route until an accident caused its withdrawal; thereafter RLST duty was its keep until 1982. Ironically, the XFs, which fall outside the scope of this book only in that they passed to London Country on 1 January 1970, proved successful there – sufficient to prompt orders for thousands of similar vehicles for the red-bus area, which became the infamous DMSs.

On New Year's Day 1973 XA 38 (JLA 38D) finds itself in need of assistance; fellow Croydon bus XA 5 (CUV 5C) is alongside. This was XA 38's last month in service, XA 5 holding out until March; both would pass to CMB in Hong Kong, there to last until 1979 (XA 5) and 1981 (XA 38).

After accident damage had finished the undistinguished career of FRM 1 (KGY 4D) in 1976, a new role was found for it in 1978 taking tourists round town under the auspices of the Round London Sightseeing Tour. This is what it is up to when captured at Tower Hill on 16 February 1978. The RLST was transferred to Victoria in 1982 and the FRM was retired the next year, serving then as now as a working exhibit at the London Transport Museum and latterly its Acton offshoot.

Chapter 4
DMSs and MDs

Such bright hopes, dashed forever by the realities of London traffic, over-sophistication and the constant meddling of politicians in things they knew nothing about. Nearly 2,000 were on order before a single example had been evaluated in service, a strategy which was almost begging to be unmasked, and so it proved. Hampered in service by gearbox failures, troublesome door interlocks and fiddly automatic fare-collection systems, the DMSs' teething troubles were not helped by spares shortages and the move of production within Leyland right in the middle of the production run.

The appearance of crew-operated DMs and the switch to the ostensibly quieter B20 variant did nothing to improve the Fleetlines' fortunes, nor could the vehicles be fitted into Aldenham's system of overhaul, so the GLC bit the bullet and commenced withdrawals mere months after the last example had been delivered. Replaced by Metrobuses and Titans, all standard DMSs were gone by 1983, but the looming changes in the way London's buses were operated forced a rethink on the B20s, not least because nobody would buy them. In the end these alone approached a normal lifespan, participating in the great push to OPO in the late 1980s and, with new engines in many cases, surviving into the devolved period of tapegrey and LBL subsidiaries; the last one, DMS 2438, was withdrawn on 20 January 1993.

The MD class of Scania BR111DH with MCW bodywork represented an attempt to forestall troubles LT was having with the DMSs; 164 entered service as crew buses on routes 36, 36A, 36B, 53 and 63 in 1976-7. While encouraging in terms of performance, the MDs were bedevilled by corrosion issues that forced many examples to fall out, and by the time the class was redeployed to OMO routes in the suburbs, eventually concentrating at the new Plumstead garage, it was decided to withdraw them too in the interests of maintaining standardisation, and the last operated on 25 June 1983.

ABOVE: The Metro-Cammell DMSs, while ostensibly identical to their Park Royal counterparts, could be discerned most readily by the aluminium beading continuing above the front upper-deck windows. DMS 1300 (MLH 300L), seen exiting London Bridge station in November 1972, had been allocated new to Victoria the previous October, its first months on the 10A being characterised by the stars on its side applied so it could eke out its evenings on the theatre-oriented Starbus service. After repaint in January 1976 it passed to Chalk Farm that December, being withdrawn from there in July 1979 – unusually as a runner, for with 79 other MCW-bodied DMSs it was dispatched to West Midlands PTE for five years' further service under the number 5530. The 10A was subsumed back into the 10 on 9 October 1976 and the 10 came off altogether in 1988; only minibus route C10, working round the backstreets, honours its memory.

OPPOSITE: The 95 was the joint debut for the DMS class, going over on 2 January 1971 with 13 Brixton vehicles, and on 19 September of that year we see DMS 31 (EGP 31J) heading southward past its home base. An uncomplicated career ensued for this vehicle; it remained at Brixton until overhaul in January 1978, being outshopped to Bexleyheath, and only one more transfer followed, to Sutton, where it spent the period spanning March 1979-July 1982. It did not survive beyond October 1982, but eleven years' service is approaching commendable for a DMS!

The terrible dreariness of the all-red livery on the DMSs did little to improve the vehicles' appeal, so from DMS 118 a white band was added where it would fit between bodyside mouldings. It brightened matters considerably, but was not to last. During July 1973 DMS 257 (JGF 257K) represents the Catford contribution to the 185, setting off from Victoria on the long and convoluted haul to Lewisham. This route had been one-manned on 12 May 1973 but the bus had been delivered new for the similar OMO conversion of the 124/A on 8 January 1972. This bus managed to secure an overhaul for itself between January-May 1979, appearing thereafter at Finchley and passing subsequently to Potters Bar, which withdrew it in December 1981; it lay in the mudheap at Ensigns for two years until scrapping in April 1984.

When it became all too clear that OMO was faltering but that the delivery schedule of DMSs was going to continue until all 1967 on order were in service, it was decided to kill two birds with one stone by operating several hundred as crew vehicles; until the delivery of purpose-built DMs with extra seating replacing the AFC equipment, standard DMSs were employed instead. One such was DMS 1598 (THM 598M), new in January 1974 and sent to Stamford Hill to replace RMs from the 149 so that its Routemasters could replace RTs elsewhere. It is seen at Liverpool Street on 5 April 1974; the following May it was transferred to Holloway, from where it was withdrawn in December 1980; via the auspices of Ensign, it was sold to KMB of Hong Kong to become 2D45, registered CN 4375.

Delivered to Bexleyheath in July 1973 as one of the first London Transport buses with the new solid white roundel, DMS 1470 (MLH 470L) is seen awaiting a driver on 20 July 1974. Other than a repaint in October 1976 and a transfer to Sidcup, that was about it for this bus's service career and after the expiry of its only seven-year CoF it ended up spending nearly twice as long as a trainer as it had taking fares! Finally in August 1992 it departed for scrap.

DMSs and MDs

1975 was the year of the DM, 460 of the sub-classification entering service in replacement of RMs and RTs. Brixton's 133 was just one of many routes to succumb, losing its RTs on 23 March 1975, and on 22 April DM 1816 (GHM 816N) looks pristine as it serves the Elephant & Castle. Brixton, however, was to re-equip with B20s, and in April 1978 DM 1816 was transferred to West Ham; its last garage was Holloway (October 1979-December 1981) before sale to PVS in October 1983.

London Transport 1970–84

The 42's main appeal is its routeing over Tower Bridge; unfortunately the stereotypical tourist would not want to risk his life on the streets anywhere to the south of that structure, which is where the 42 wandered on its way to Camberwell Green. DMS 2109 (KJD 109P) was one of a handful put into service at Camberwell in July 1976 while the 42 was still double-deck operated; this sunny 26 August 1976 shot taken at Aldgate shows the attractive white-top livery to full advantage. The usual miserly seven years' service afforded by its CoF ensued, DMS 2109 coming off service in May 1983, but a twist developed when its rotting remains were dragged out of the mire at Purfleet and revived as Bexleybus 96, operating that benighted network from 16 January 1988 until February 1990; even then it was kept on, bizarrely receiving an LBL-corporate repaint over its front only to serve as a very short-term loan at Merton while that garage's DMSs were loaned to Stockwell for the 196. A much smarter livery followed when DMS 2109 became the property of Big Bus, and it took those colours to Philadelphia.

The B20 DMS was billed as the 'quiet bus', which it most emphatically was not, being likened instead to a hairdryer. May 1978 sees DMS 2311 (THX 311S) at Mansion House as one of Brixton's new complement for the 50 and 95. Managing to get an overhaul in before treatment of the B20s was cancelled, DMS 2311 was outshopped to Sutton in August 1982. Re-engining with a powerful Iveco lump in March 1988 was followed by its transfer on 29 September 1990 to the Colliers Wood outstation (AA), the operations and buses of which were absorbed by Merton in March 1991, but for the last three months of its life (August-November 1991) it returned to Brixton, its first home.

Overhaul spread the early DMSs far and wide from their original bases; although body and chassis could not be separated in works, the length of time it took to turn the buses around meant that they had to be replaced at their source garages instantly rather than by a works-float bus coming out to replace them as with previous generations. Thus, DMS 85 (EGP 85J) new to Cricklewood for the 32 and spending 1976-7 at West Ham, was overhauled between February and June 1978; after seven months at Sidcup it was transferred to Bromley, under whose stewardship it is seen in this 6 September 1979 shot at Bromley South. Spells at Holloway, Wood Green, Edmonton and Thornton Heath took it up to withdrawal in February 1982. Compare the headlights with Bromley stablemate DMS 1471 (MLH 471L) messing up the headway straight behind it. This MCW-bodied July 1973 delivery had come to Bromley from West Ham in April 1975, but would not undergo overhaul, serving at Sutton between September 1979 (when Bromley lost its DMSs) and June 1980; training work, principally from Edmonton, became its lot until May 1983 when withdrawal was followed inevitably by scrapping.

DMS 843 (TGX 843M) looks adequately cared for in this 3 June 1980 shot at Harrow-on-the-Hill, but look what's coming up behind it: one of the Metrobuses that would be replacing it from Alperton. Sure enough, the Fleetline was transferred to Wood Green and survived only for as long as its remaining ticket would permit, which was eight more months. At seven years of age, it was perfectly good enough for further service in a quieter environment, which it accomplished with, in turn, Supreme Coaches, Arlington Motors, Queen City and Wealden Omnibus; its final years were spent in Belgium.

ABOVE: The DM class inevitably fell foul of popular opinion, but that much-needed spot of flexibility was ensured for as long as the buses still had life in them by fitting them with a powered Almex E cab-edge baseplate and a signboard instructing the passengers to 'PAY DRIVER'/'PAY CONDUCTOR' as fit, and reclassifying them D. As AFC usage had been discontinued by this time, there is no reason why the DMS code couldn't have been used, but D 1220 (KUC 220P) fits in quite happily as an OMO bus as it reposes outside its home garage, Sutton, on 4 June 1981. Its crew days had been spent at Hanwell on the 207; as a D it would work from Sutton until October 1982, after which Ensigns transformed it into an unusual convertible open-topper, in which format it operated with a variety of Welsh and West Country firms until 1993.

OPPOSITE: Despite the heavy inroads made into the DMS class as early as 1979, the majority of the first 367 survived to undergo overhaul and the four-year CoF it bestowed, giving them an almost-respectable eleven years in total – actually, quite a bit more than can be expected of today's buses; and with adequate seating capacity, comfort and blind provision at that. Maybe the poor old DMS is vindicated at last! Originally a Shepherd's Bush motor, DMS 6 (EGP 6J) was outshopped from Aldenham overhaul in April 1978 to Fulwell, moving to Chalk Farm in March 1979 and also serving from Putney at one point, but in March 1982 it was transferred to Holloway, whose route 239 it is seen working at Euston on 24 May. Neither DMS 6 nor the 239 would survive the massive purge of 4 September 1982.

ABOVE: Wandsworth was early to the B20 DMS, operating them on the 44 and 295; DMS 2494 (THX 494S) began working from there in April 1982 after overhaul following four years at Enfield. Never have the gasholders at Wandsworth looked so shiny and cheerful when photographed as the backdrop to this unremarkable Fleetline on 28 October 1983! Replaced four months later by an influx of Ms, DMS 2494 headed south to Thornton Heath, but it was not until much later that it was to become one of the last three DMSs in service; having been transferred to Croydon on 14 March 1992, it was withdrawn from there that October alongside DMS 2480, leaving DMS 2438 alone to carry the class into 1993.

OPPOSITE: The great redeployment of the B20 DMS fleet saw Wandle District restocked entirely with the type over 1982 and into 1983; DMS 2304 (THX 304S), new to Brixton in January 1978, was overhauled between July and October 1982 and outshopped to Sutton. After 23 April 1983 the 93 became one of its regular haunts, this last of Sutton's crew routes going over to OMO on that day. It is seen on 23 September ascending Putney Hill, and would remain based here until withdrawal in May 1992. Training work under the DMT classification and with a yellow front took it into the millennium, but only just.

Heading through New Cross on 12 March 1976, MD 2 (KJD 202P) is familiarising Peckham's RM drivers with the first of 111 Metropolitans shortly to enter service on the 36 group. Attractive in its white-top livery and with a bit more visual interest around the lower half than the contemporary DMS, the MD class attracted acclaim immediately for its superior performance; pity that the testbed chosen was not in any way appropriate for doored buses, even those speeded up by a conductor. MD 2 spent five years at Peckham, barring a brief posting to Plumstead in April 1980 and receiving a red repaint during that year, before transferring to the new Plumstead garage upon its opening on 31 October 1981. However, Plumstead's first intake of Titans edged it out as early as September 1982, and it became Reading Transport 401 the following year.

DMSs and MDs

The 36B was by far the senior partner in the 36 trio, descending from a tram-replacement route and only numbered in the 36 series later for convenience. Upon its conversion from RM on 13 April 1976 it required 44 crew MDs, one of which is Peckham's MD 53 (KJD 253P) seen in Downham Way on 26 June 1976. It lasted at Peckham only as long as the 36 group retained Metropolitans, transferring in February 1980 to Plumstead and on 31 October 1981 to the new Plumstead. Withdrawn in September 1982, it was scrapped by C. F. Booth the following July.

London Transport 1970–84

ABOVE: The problems suffered by doored buses keeping to time in central London were compounded by their mechanical unreliability and the spares shortage, so in 1980 the 36 group reverted to RMs and the MDs began redeploying to Plumstead. The 122, at that time the longest route in London and only having lost its RTs in 1978, became their main employ, and on 5 July 1980 MD 22 (KJD 222P) is seen at its Crystal Palace terminus ready for the long haul to Bexleyheath Garage. Six months later it was repainted, one of the small number of MDs to receive this treatment, and passed to the new Plumstead on 31 October 1981; withdrawal followed in September 1982 and scrapping ensued in September 1983.

OPPOSITE: The last fifty MDs were allocated to New Cross to convert the busy trunk route 53 from RM from 8 January 1977; about to make the protected right-hand turn from Westminster Bridge into Whitehall, avoiding having to go round Parliament Square, is MD 156 (OUC 156R) that September. Like most of the MDs, it gravitated to the new Plumstead, from where it was withdrawn in January 1983; the scrapman beckoned in 1984.

London Transport 1970–84

ABOVE: The fate of most Fleetlines and Metropolitans - but six-and-a-half-year-old MD 100 (OUC 100R) doesn't look particularly near the end of its life, and nor do the two DMs of similar vintage espied next to it upon Dick Riley's 7 June 1983 visit to Ensign's Purfleet premises. MD 100, veteran of both Plumsteads after starting at New Cross, was sold to Reading Transport and is still extant today, while DM 1197 (KUC 197P), late of Wood Green, and DM 1193 (KUC 193P), last known at Potters Bar, would soon be off to China Motor Bus in Hong Kong.

OPPOSITE: Not all MDs remained crew buses when the 36 group and 53 reverted to RM at the turn of the 1980s; a number remained at Peckham to be fitted for OMO and allocated to the 78 in place of DMSs. This took place on 24 February 1980, and on 20 September 1981 at Aldgate MD 21 (KJD 221P) shows us what the MD looked like in all-red and with a 'PAY DRIVER'/'PAY CONDUCTOR' plate fitted. Moving to Plumstead the following month, MD 21 was among the last to be withdrawn thanks to a late recertification, but in April 1983 was taken out of service, passing after two months to a coach firm in Devon.

Chapter 5

Metrobuses and Titans

What came to be known as 'second-generation' OMO double-deckers, the M and T classes proved successful and reliable, and carried London Transport through its bitterest period in which its operations were separated and then sold. Developed as an all-British competitor to Leyland's near-monopoly, the Metrobus grew to 1,440 members in London, plus two mark IIs; later came 14 second-hand examples and 29 leased mark IIs when tendering blew apart London Transport's unified image and commercial operations were attempted. Inherited by seven successors to LBL, the M remained in service until low-floor buses finally began to replace them at the turn of the century; the last ran on 11 September 2004 from Potters Bar.

The Titan's birth was not as smooth; production looked doomed at one point when Leyland determined to close the Park Royal plant it had inherited from AEC, and until construction was resumed at Workington, Titans were outnumbered almost two to one by Metrobuses. Further orders took numbers up to 1125, but fewer than 40 were sold outside London and the model was cancelled, the last examples arriving in October 1984. Participating in the OPO push, the T class remained intact until 1992 when sales commenced; the general concentration of the type in the eastern half of town caused the survivors to pass to the locally-based successors to LBL, two of which were Stagecoach subsidiaries and one Go-Ahead. The former's Titans operated until October 2001 and London Central had the privilege of operating the last one of all on 19 June 2003. Both Metrobus and Titan figured heavily in the operation of independents in London, as did the DMSs before them, and in the same respect served faithfully with subsequent operators throughout Britain and the world.

Metrobuses and Titans

ABOVE: Long before the Heathrow Express rail link, there was Airbus, a cheaper and arguably more comfortable alternative to the Piccadilly Line to and from the airport. Seventeen Stamford Brook-based Metrobuses formed the complement on the two routes (A1 to Victoria and A2 to Russell Square), fitted with luggage racks on the lower deck. M 441 (GYE 441W), departing Victoria on 26 May 1982, shows off the experimental repainting of the M's frontal panels red, which practice later spread to the rest of the fleet. Eased off this work by newer Ms in 1984, M 441 subsequently worked from Norbiton, Stamford Brook (again, but as a normal-service bus), Cricklewood, Edgware and Croydon before privatisation froze it as a Cowie-group bus; within this group (renamed to Arriva in 1998) it crossed the river again to work at Tottenham and Clapton before ending its career with Leaside Travel.

OPPOSITE: London Transport and its splintered successors were able to get over a quarter of a century out of their Metrobuses, something unlikely ever to be even approached nowadays. Exemplifying the original M-class look with its black-painted aluminium-barred radiator grille is M 207 (BYX 207V), new to Stonebridge as a crew-operated bus for the 18 but later transferred to Fulwell, on whose 90B it is seen operating in Richmond on 8 March 1982; the correct 'PLEASE PAY AS YOU ENTER' transfers have not yet been applied. It was withdrawn from Merton, by that time a London General garage, in August 2000; its fundamentals allowed Stratford Blue's examples to buy some more time for themselves and the rest was broken up by PVS in 2003.

London Transport 1970–84

ABOVE: Eyebrows were raised in August 1982 when six Ms were deployed to a garage unlikely ever to receive them in the district-based means of allocation prevalent at the time, but Sidcup's route 51 was selected to evaluate the M, T and remaining DMSs alongside each other so as to determine what to keep ordering. Green Street Green, the terminus of the 51 until 4 September 1982, is the location of M 802 (KYV 802X) in the second half of July; a Titan could be relied on to follow on the next running number in the series, and a DMS on the one after that. Its work done, M 802 was transferred to Muswell Hill in May 1986 to convert the 134 from RM, and in November 1988 moved to Holloway, there to spend ten years until inter-Metroline transfers took it to Willesden and then Harrow Weald. After sale in September 1999 it lingered in London, first with Connex Buses as a trainer and then with Imperial. It was scrapped in 2007.

OPPOSITE: Norbiton was the second London Transport garage to take on production Ms, re-equipping thus during the summer of 1979, and on 10 August 1982 at Wimbledon M 72 (WYW 72T) exemplifies the 131's usual stock. After overhaul over the cusp of 1983/84 it returned to Norbiton but was reallocated to Potters Bar when the Kingston Bus operations were decimated on 29 September 1990, there to work until August 1998 other than a brief spell at Holloway. It did not last the century out, succumbing to the torches of PVS.

The 91, a long and not exceptionally interesting straight line down the Great West Road, had often been the testbed for experimental vehicles due to its proximity to Chiswick Works; at the end of 1979 it was converted from DMS to M and the following June was reallocated from Turnham Green to Stamford Brook; M 142 (BYX 142V) was one of the buses to have made that move and on 28 October 1983 it was still performing daily on the 91 alone, in this shot having just arrived at the Wandsworth Garage terminus. M 142's career was unremarkable; it moved to Cricklewood in November 1987, Edgware in December 1998 (though its work at Cricklewood included Edgware routes for some years) and was withdrawn in August 1999, only a few months short of its 20th birthday. A short period with Town & Country Buses was followed by scrapping in December 2001.

Battersea's only OMO route was the 39, which received Ms 846-9/55-60/5-9 in May 1983. 5 February 1984 is a Sunday, so the route is going no further towards town than Battersea Garage, but M 860 (OJD 860Y) is still displaying the panel for the full route to Victoria. Battersea's closure on 2 November 1985 took the 39 and M 860 to Victoria; the bus moved on to Wandsworth in February 1987 and to Hanwell the month after, to work on the 207. Acton Tram Depot inherited this work on 6 March 1993 and M 860 remained there until February 2000; PVS broke it up two months later.

ABOVE: Burned badly by the DMS, London Transport resolved to regain as much input into the manufacturing of its vehicles as it had lost when it abandoned the FRM, and the result was the elegant and ultimately successful Leyland Titan. Known initially as project B15, the demonstrator, NHG 732P, was deployed to Chalk Farm and the 24 at the start of 1976. On Sundays it worked the 3, still as a crew-operated vehicle, and it is at this route's Crystal Palace terminus that the prototype Titan is seen on 15 May 1977. It toured the country after its LT service, settling with Fishwick and Gagg during the 1980s and working in Liverpool in the 1990s with Village and then with MTL North; it survives today in preservation, though under the Northern Ireland registration UJI 6314.

OPPOSITE: Tower District's spread of inner-London garages began to receive Titans in 1982, Camberwell's 196 being a slightly different case in that it was a straight OMO conversion from Routemaster. With more than a little attention from nesting birds, T 498 (KYV 498X) climbs through West Norwood on 16 May 1983. The 196 bounced back and forth in the ensuing decade, even at one point seeing a second combination of Camberwell and Titans, and T 498 was similarly to cross the river repeatedly, working from North Street (April 1984), Bow (September 1988), Bromley (September 1997) and Leyton (May 1998) before taking up at Barking in October 2000 to finish its career. After withdrawal in February 2001 it spent five years with Freeway Coaches in Derbyshire, but was scrapped in 2006.

ABOVE: T 859 (A859 SUL) spent all but the last two months of its London career at Catford; new in October 1983, it was sold in July 1998 after the twin indignities of privatisation of its operator (September 1994) and conversion to single-door (January 1998, preceding transfer to Bromley). It is seen when new in winter sunshine on Dog Kennel Hill on the 185. T 859 saw the millennium in as a Stagecoach Devon General bus operating in Torbay under the Bayline banner, and in 2001 passed to Isle Coaches of Owston Ferry; by 2006 it had moved again to Orbit Travel in Leicester.

OPPOSITE: The 180's majority Plumstead allocation, inherited from its predecessor with MDs, was converted to crew T at the beginning of 1983 with Titans like T 688 (OHV 688Y) seen swinging into the route's southern stand at Catford Garage, which provided the remaining three buses (which were still RMs but would soon be replaced by Ts themselves). The upheavals of 2 November 1985 rendered T 688 too new for Plumstead's revised mechanical standard and the bus moved to Peckham, but further changes saw it cross the river in November 1988 and strike up at Muswell Hill, not historically a Titan operator; nor were Finchley (21 July 1990) or Chalk Farm (October 1990-March 1991). Displaced from a second spell at Finchley by Ms in October 1992, T 688 formed part of a drive to update the age profile at Barking and spent the remainder of its career there, weathering privatisation under Stagecoach and coming off service in June 1997. Thereafter it spent the rest of the decade at Stagecoach East Kent, after which it operated with Rennies of Dunfermline (August 2001) and Williams of Ancaster (September 2005) before sale for scrap in December 2008.

London Transport 1970–84

ABOVE: Just on its way out of Aldgate bus station on the same day is T 421 (KYV 421X), well settled at Camberwell by this time, though it had started at Loughton where double-deck operation was ruthlessly expunged after the cuts of 4 September 1982. Following its displacement from the 42 by newer Titans not long after this photograph was taken, T 421 worked from Poplar, West Ham, Hornchurch, Upton Park and Bow, its spells at the last four garages as a roving cover for mechanical work on fellow Ts. After that work was done it served at Plumstead and Ash Grove before spending the cusp of 1991/2 as a DMS replacement at distant Croydon, moving on to Catford and then returning to the East End to round out its comparatively short career at Barking. Between April 1993 and April 2000 it served in Liverpool with Merseybus.

OPPOSITE: London Transport's efforts to decentralise its bus operations spawned eight districts, of which Tower was one; its chosen type was Titans and buses like T 534 (KYV 534X) arrived in 1982 for Clapton's route 22A. It looks perfectly settled in this Aldgate shot of 14 February 1984, but in 1985 Tower District was deleted and Clapton placed in Abbey, whose modern OMO type was Metrobuses. And even after the 22A thus went over to Ms, a surfeit of Titans following heavy losses in the first rounds of tendering forced the 22A to resume T operation anyway! The 22A is now part of the 242, while T 534 had a most varied career, spending time at West Ham, Clapton (again, for the reasons above), Ash Grove, Croydon, Brixton and New Cross before heading to Liverpool in August 1993 as one of more than two hundred Titans to join the fleet of Merseybus. It was withdrawn as an Arriva Merseyside bus in April 2000 and scrapped in May.

Chapter 6
RFs

The toughest small bus ever built, the RF class comprised 700 MCW-bodied AEC Regals. Bought to replace front-engined Ts and TDs, the RFs entered service between 1951-3 and could soon be seen at all corners of the system, not only where double-deckers would not fit but on prestige Green Line routes. By the time this book's coverage starts, 484 RFs had just passed to London Country, but a large number remained in town. Only in 1976 were serious thoughts to their replacement put into action, and in the end they declined to a recertified hard core based on Kingston and operating out of that garage due to the inability of the pits there to accommodate Swifts. The last RFs were withdrawn with a flourish on 31 March 1979.

After spinning off London Country on 1 January 1970, LT was left with 233 RFs. Despite overhauls restarting in 1971, withdrawals commenced in 1973 with DMSs and SMSs replacing them as fit; however, some roads could not accommodate these larger modern vehicles. On 20 January 1974 RF 326 (MLL 963) is seen reposing in Norbiton garage, its home between June 1973 and April 1976. The 201 was converted to BL not long after this RF was withdrawn and the route itself disappeared in 1978; RF 326, however, thrived and is one of the very large number of preserved RFs to be enjoyed on the rally circuit today.

At Shepperton, along the outer end of the 237 route, we see Hounslow's RF 356 (MLL 993) on 6 October 1975. This one was withdrawn the following April and scrapped before 1976 was out.

On the same day and on the other side of the road from the previous picture is another Kingston steed, RF 371 (MXX 13), in the last year of a 24-year service career that had taken it via Merton, Norbiton, Sutton, Croydon, Bromley, New Cross, Bromley again and Uxbridge before landing at Kingston in December 1971 after its fourth and final overhaul. RF 371 was withdrawn in September 1976 and sold that November.

On 25 March 1977, two months before it was withdrawn, RF 442 (MXX 419) is seen loading up at Hounslow bus station on the 237; this route would undergo a surprising transformation a year later that saw it become an RM route, swapping its main effort to Shepherd's Bush with the 117. RF 442 is also preserved.

Chapter 7

Merlins and Swifts

Pity the poor Merlins and Swifts. For all the brave new world of the Reshaping Plan, London Transport totally failed to grasp that the minimum return expected by the typical bus passenger upon boarding was a seat and the freedom to prepare his or her payment in his or her own time. Not to mention a bus that wouldn't break down more times than not over trivialities like water ingress, body distortion, underpowered noisy engines and overcomplicated gearbox interlocks. Thus the attempt to shoehorn Londoners from seated, served comfort to standee cattle-truck operation as endured on the Continent flopped horribly. The MB family was gone within five years save for Red Arrow work (which was short-hop enough for commuter types to be used to being piled in like livestock, just as on the trains that had brought them to the railheads from which the Red Arrows emanated), and the Swifts lasted little longer; all had gone by 1981.

ABOVE: The 99, an unhurried wander across the Bostall Heath woodlands, was converted from RT to MB on 24 January 1970, and on 7 April 1973 Plumstead's MB 625 (AML 625H), a single-doored conventional OMO example, is seen at work. It only ever worked from this garage, having come in new in August 1969 and leaving in March 1977; it managed to escape destruction while operating in Belfast, but was broken up in 1982.

OPPOSITE: On 25 August 1971 Camberwell's MB 182 (VLW 182G) serves the Royal Mint, its driver hoping to take on similar coin from southbound punters. The 42 had lost RTs for Merlins on 24 January 1970. After a year at Walworth as Red Arrow MBA 182, this bus lost the 'A' to its code and became a Camberwell lifer as a conventional OMO bus albeit with dual doors. After withdrawal, it languished at Radlett Aerodrome until 1980.

Born to Red Arrow work, MBA 567 (AML 567H) filtered onto this type of operation after just seven months as flat-fare MBS 567. When seen at Westminster on 14 May 1976 it had been a Victoria bus for six years and would remain so for another five, succumbing to a National 2 in May 1981.

The 132 represented a 'normal' RT-to-Swift conversion, taking its single-doored SMs on 18 April 1970; SM 20 (AML 20H), being looked over by a couple of kids outside its home garage, Bexleyheath, that December, was one of them. Although the 132 suffered under DMSs sufficient to have to revert to SM operation towards the end of the decade, SM 20 had transferred away long before that, serving at Fulwell, Poplar, Catford, Poplar again (after overhaul), Peckham and finally Southall until September 1980. Amazingly, it could still be found in service nearly twenty years later, its Maltese operator not worrying about the type's perceived unreliability.

ABOVE: The running-number holders on Peckham's SMS 695 (EGN 695J) have been repositioned from behind the emergency-exit door to just behind the cab, unfortunately straight over the relief band. The reputation of Peckham, however, was even then ominous enough that a driver or engineer could not quite count himself safe traversing that extra few feet once out of the safety of the cab, even when on the garage premises as in this 15 February 1976 shot! The P3's operation with SMSs represented a demotion from XAs, and likewise was the transfer of SMS 695 from bucolic Loughton in February 1973. It did not even last out its seven-year CoF, sale for scrap ensuing in March 1978.

OPPOSITE: Before long the Red Arrow services started to take examples of the SMS after Merlins fell out, forming a mixed allocation. SMS 160 (EGN 160J) had actually been around quite a bit before pitching up at Victoria in May 1979, serving since delivery in June 1970 at Enfield (on the 107), Turnham Green (the E-routes), Bromley (the 227), Hornchurch and Norbiton. The huge roundel offers a cheerful welcome to potential customers of this Swift as it heads for Waterloo on 26 June 1979 for what in retrospect seems like an absolute bargain fare of 12p. SMS 160 did not stick around to wait for the National 2s to usurp it, departing for scrap in July 1980.

Merlins and Swifts

London Transport 1970–84

Merlins and Swifts

ABOVE: The Red Arrows' last year under Merlins and Swifts is epitomised on 15 February 1980 by Hackney's SMS 700 (JGF 700K), captured leaving the Waterloo stand that would eventually be transformed into the Red Arrows' very own garage. Very much a latecomer to the 500-series routes, this Swift had spent the majority of its career at Harrow Weald, though starting at Turnham Green and preceding its transfer to Hackney with spells at Elmers End, Harrow Weald (again) and Walworth. It was withdrawn from Walworth in July 1981 as one of the very last SMSs in service.

OPPOSITE: Over on the north-west edge of London the Swift family could still count itself in substantial numbers by the turn of the 1980s, working from Edgware and Harrow Weald; it is to the latter that SMS 295 (EGN 295J) was allocated when espied on 3 August 1979 in Ruislip. This bus had also done its share of wandering in its decade of service, operating from Elmers End, Croydon and Thornton Heath, where it spent the majority of its career, even managing to pack in an overhaul. This was what took it to Harrow Weald, and after ejection from here by an LS in September 1979 it would spend its last year at Edgware, being stood down finally in November 1980.

ABOVE: By 5 May 1980, when Thornton Heath's SMS 545 (EGN 545J) was pictured looking out of its home garage, the route number on Merlins' and Swifts' blinds had been swapped from the offside to the nearside to aid intending passengers. The 115 was probably more suited to standee single-decks than most, operating a convoluted path through swathes of south London; it had gone over to SMS from RT on 2 January 1971 and DMSs would only take over on 17 July 1980, a year after which the route was incorporated into adjacent services. SMS 545 began that year at Holloway, working subsequently at Palmers Green before transfer to Thornton Heath in September 1977; its time at this garage included an overhaul. Despite withdrawal in July 1980 it was reinstated at Uxbridge until the end of the year and sold for scrap straight after.

OPPOSITE: Edgware saw out the SM family on non-Red Arrow work, gathering a number that were replaced first by DMSs and then by Metrobuses as 1980 spooled out. On 3 June that year SMS 317 (EGN 317J) is seen in Harrow-on-the-Hill on the 186. Having served since delivery at the tail end of 1970 at Thornton Heath, Peckham and Harrow Weald before coming to Edgware in August 1979, it would reach the end of the road with the rest in December 1980 and meet the fate of the majority.

Chapter 8

MSs and LSs

A handful of routes remained that could not traverse roads served by double-deckers due to height or width, or did not enjoy enough custom to merit a double-decker. After dabbling in Metro-Scanias (six MSs) and six Leyland Nationals (LSs), London Transport picked up a cancelled order for the latter from Venezuela and found that they were substantially more reliable than Merlins or Swifts. When DMSs began falling out at the end of the 1970s, the Leyland National could be relied upon to be delivered in time to replace them in the short term. Although not what you would call terribly interesting, the LS served out the decade expected of full-size single-deckers and retired quietly, though the 69 National 2s bought for Red Arrow work in 1981 underwent Greenway conversion long after the period covered by this book and survived until 2002.

ABOVE: The white-top livery that adorned the MSs and LSs was a bright spot in the decade that good taste otherwise forgot. The first of what would eventually be a fleet of 506 Leyland Nationals, LS 1 (TGY 101M) and partner share the S2's stand at Clapton Pond in November 1974. When the S2's trial came to an end both moved to Hounslow to join the newer examples going into service there, and lasted until 1985. After a spell as Ensignbus 502, LS 1 was broken up in 1990.

OPPOSITE: Despite having used and returned the Metro-Scania demonstrator VWD 451H without taking any more, London Transport gave the model a second try with a solid order for six to be evaluated alongside an equal number of Leyland Nationals in the interests of Merlin and Swift replacement where single-decks were still needed. Thus on 7 May 1974 is seen Dalston's MS 2 (PGC 202L) at Bromley-by-Bow, nine months into what would prove to be little under three years of service. After service it spent time in the experimental shop at Chiswick and is now preserved.

ABOVE: Hounslow was the recipient of all fifty of the order placed in 1976 for Nationals diverted from a cancelled export order for Venezuela. LS 26 (KJD 526P) is seen at Hampton Station on 25 March 1977, on a short-working of the 111 route. An uneventful career followed; overhauled between June and September 1983, LS 26 was outshopped to Bromley and lasted there until December 1989.

OPPOSITE: A popular fixture on the rally circuit today, LS 103 (OJD 903R) was new to Bromley in August 1977 and by 12 October 1979, when this shot was taken at Bromley South station, had taken over the 61, 126 and 138 from DMSs as well as the 227 for which it had been delivered. After overhaul (April-July 1982) it was sent to Elmers End for the 12A, passing with the route to Croydon upon Elmers End's closure on 25 October 1986. It was withdrawn in July 1990.

ABOVE: In the decade after this photograph was taken, one of London Transport's stated aims was to bring a bus to within 400 metres of every Londoner's residence, but somehow this wasn't what they had in mind! On 1 July 1980 an otherwise uneventful journey by Elmers End's LS 66 (OJD 866R) was interrupted by this unfortunate charge straight through the living room of a house in Rectory Road, not far from Dick Riley's Beckenham home. The bus was invariably repaired and went on to a more eventful career than enjoyed by most LT Nationals, serving after overhaul at Muswell Hill, Holloway, Bow, Catford and Ash Grove. It was sold in July 1993 to the Anti-Vivisection Society, of all people; hadn't the bus already tried to disembowel itself once?

OPPOSITE: The National 2 was physically larger and more imposing-looking than the original, and came at you with a thunderous roar! Probably too many were purchased for the Red Arrow network, which began a slow decline, and by 1983 something had to be done about the spare buses stacking up. Stockwell's P4, born as a minibus route, was selected, having undergone an extension which brought it into the path of more passengers, and on 7 March 1983 LS 488 (GUW 488W) doesn't look at all out of place. However, the P4 was one of the first routes to be lost on tender and, after a period out of service which incorporated an overhaul by British Leyland at Nottingham, LS 488 was transferred to Holloway to take over the 210. Unusually, it was returned to Red Arrow work in 1989 but kept the extra seating it had been given when converted for the P4; even so, it did not form part of the 41 LSs converted to National Greenways and was privatised with the assets of London Northern. Under MTL ownership it was sent to Liverpool in January 1995.

Chapter 9
BSs and BLs

Even the sturdy RF couldn't be depended on for much more than an epic quarter-century, and by the mid-1970s London Transport was having to eye contemporary small buses of much the same capacity; having experimented with a Seddon Pennine, LT plumped for the Bristol LH. Seventeen short examples (BSs) and 95 long (BLs) entered service in 1976-7. Neither model was in the same league as the RF, and the BS variant in particular was soon sold and forgotten, but the BL class lingered throughout the 1980s; quite a few more had been ordered than were really needed, but enough survived to go through overhaul and even pass to one of the devolved subsidiaries, Metroline, which operated the last route (251) until 1990.

The BS class of Bristol LHSs were among the funniest-looking creatures ever operated by LT, retaining the chassis of the longer version but cutting it off at the back. Six were ordered in 1975 to add more capacity to the successful minibus service C11; six more followed at the end of 1976 for the B1, P4 and W9, and here at Bromley North on 3 March 1977 is Bromley's BS 9 (OJD 9R). The white numberplate was unusual in itself, only the LSs otherwise wearing them. Also seeing service at Stockwell and Enfield, BS 9 lasted only until 1980 and it left the fleet the following year.

Only a month after the last RFs operated, Kingston's BL 46 (OJD 46R) noses out of the side entrance of that garage on 27 April 1979. The BLs were about right for the longer-range services leaving the GLC area for the leafier edges of Surrey, or at least were before cuts started taking buses out of those regions altogether if they could not be provided more cheaply by equivalent London Country services. New in September 1976, BL 46 was transferred (after a repaint) to Bromley in December 1980 and to Croydon in March 1982 but was withdrawn that June. It subsequently served in Scotland for Grampian and in Guernsey, but was scrapped as the new millennium commenced.

Chapter 11

Beyond

If passengers thought they had it bad by the time 1984 dawned, they hadn't seen anything yet. The rest of the decade was characterised by mass OPO conversions, Routemaster withdrawals and worst of all, the commencement of the destruction of London Transport itself. 'Cowboy' operators of sharply reduced quality began to take over services under the banner of tendering, their choice of superannuated vehicles taking the future of British bus manufacturing to the brink. Perhaps this debacle will be dissected in a further volume.

One of the niceties to fall by the wayside as London Transport began its slow decline was standardisation of type operation; at Lewisham during the summer of 1986 are Leyland Titan T 550 (NUW 550Y) and new Leyland Olympian L 27 (C27 CHM), both allocated to the new Plumstead garage constructed in 1981. Having replaced its MDs with Ts in 1982-83, Plumstead then rotated its entire allocation for older examples that would be mechanically standard for the garages to which they would be transferred after Ls took over. The Ls were LBL's last new buses, a free-for-all reigning thereafter as tendered concerns stocked up with second-hand buses. Mercifully, we do not have to see what befell the 178 in 1988 – its transfer to the infamous Bexleybus.

Chapter 10

FSs

A decade and a half before they would become the scourge of passengers up and down the country, van-based minibuses were just an experiment aimed at tapping outlying areas unable to be served by proper buses. The FS class made its debut in 1972 on just such a service, the Hampstead Garden Suburb Dial-A-Ride. This was successful enough to sprout proper stops as route H2, and soon was to be followed by four more minibus services. A second generation of FSs replaced the first in 1981, and three final examples popped up in 1985. None could be counted on to survive long, but they embedded the minibus concept in bus operations forever, for good or ill.

Less the bane of enthusiasts today than a clever gimmick and a genuinely successful experiment in attracting more passengers from hitherto inaccessible areas, the van-based minibus is here represented by Strachans-bodied Ford Transit FS 7 (MLK 707L) in Dulwich on 7 October 1972. Before withdrawal in September 1979 (making its seven years a fairly decent innings for a van!) it had also operated out of Bromley (for the B1) and Potters Bar (the PB1) as well as its original P4 from Stockwell. Even then, more work beckoned, with Clintona of Brentwood.